HOUGHTON MIFFLIN
Reading
A Legacy of Literacy

Nature:
Friend and Foe

HOUGHTON MIFFLIN

BOSTON • MORRIS PLAINS, NJ

California • Colorado • Georgia • Illinois • New Jersey • Texas

Design, Art Management and Page Production: Kirchoff/Wohlberg, Inc.

ILLUSTRATION CREDITS
4-21 John F. Martin. 26, 39 Mike DiGiorgio. 40-57 Dave Kramer.

PHOTOGRAPHY CREDITS
22 (bkgd) Corbis. 22 Jacques Jangoux/Tony Stone Images. 23 Galen
Rowell/Corbis. 24-5 J. Messerschmidt/Bruce Coleman, Inc. 24 (i) Gale
Powell/Corbis. 26-7 Macduff Everton/Corbis. 28 (l) USGS. 28 (r) Don
Duckson/VU. 29 David Weintraub/Photo Researchers. 31 Jim Sugar/
Corbis. 32 (t) Steve Strickland/VU. 32 (b) Jim Sugar/Corbis. 33 Vince
Streano/Corbis. 34 RGK Photography/Tony Stone Images. 34 (i) Alan
Detrick/Photo Researchers. 35 Nik Wheeler/Corbis. 36 Lowell Georgia/
Corbis. 37 (t) Bob Rowan/Corbis. 37 (b) Tom McHugh/Photo Researchers.
38 Gerald Corsi/VU. 39 (t) Corbis. 39 (b) Steve Strickland/VU. 40 Robert
Estall/Corbis. 57 Robert Estall/Corbis.

Printed in U.S.A.

ISBN: 0-618-04404-3

789-VH-05 04 03 02

Nature:
Friend and Foe

Contents

Peter's Harvest

by Anne Sibley O'Brien

illustrated by John F. Martin

Strategy Focus

How will Peter learn the family tradition of harvesting wild rice? As you read, stop and **summarize** each part of the story.

A rich, smoky smell rose from Peter's plate. Peter looked closely at the grains of rice. Each grain had split open. They looked as if they had golden wings. Peter tasted a spoonful. He let the nutty flavor roll around in his mouth.

"Is it good?" asked his mother.

Peter nodded. This rice was better than good. For Peter, it was special in a way that was hard to describe.

5

Peter had been eating this kind of rice his whole life. But at this meal, he was eating rice he had helped to pick, or *harvest*. Maybe that was why the rice seemed so wonderful.

Wild rice was the name English-speaking people used for this food. To them, the thin grain looked like rice. Peter's people, the Ojibwe (Oh-**jib**-way), called it *manoomin*. Manoomin was a grass. It grew wild, and its seeds gave life.

Hundreds of years ago, the Ojibwe came to the lands around the upper Great Lakes. Wild grass grew in the lakes and rivers. The Ojibwe learned that grains from the grass could be made into good food. They learned when it was best to harvest the grain and how to prepare the grain for eating.

Ojibwe Homelands

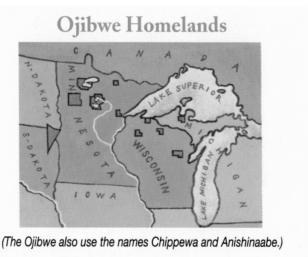

(The Ojibwe also use the names Chippewa and Anishinaabe.)

As parents passed down their learning to their children, they also told stories about manoomin. They told how their great hero, Manabozho (Man-a-**bo**-zo), had helped them find it.

Today, many Ojibwe live in the homelands of their ancestors. Some Ojibwe still harvest manoomin in the old way.

Autumn / Winter   Spring

Throughout the fall and winter, grains of wild rice lie in the mud under water. In the spring, the melting snows bring floods. The moving water stirs up the mud. The rice grains begin to send out roots. As the roots grow into plants, they begin climbing toward the sun.

By early summer, the stalks are poking up from the water. Flowers appear. The stalks and leaves grow taller and taller. By late summer, the plants are three feet above the water.

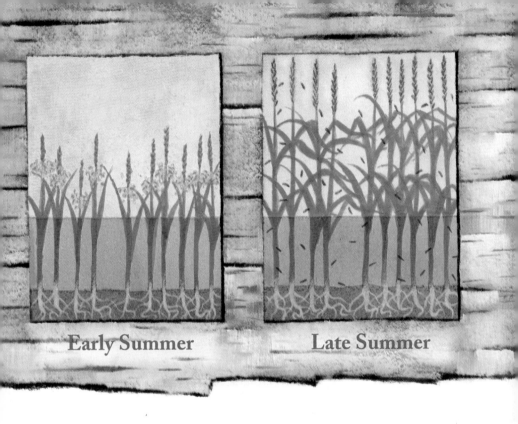

Early Summer   Late Summer

The flowers have formed dark red seeds. These seeds are the grains. When the seeds are ripe, they fall off into the water. They drift down into the mud where they will grow in the next spring.

The ripe seeds are ready to fall in late August and early September. That is the time for harvesting.

This season, Peter's family drove to their usual spot for ricing. Peter looked out at the lake. It was like a field of grass. He looked into the bright blue sky. He saw a few ducks flying in the distance. They were enjoying harvest time too.

Peter's mother and grandfather took the canoe out. They had been ricing together ever since Peter could remember. Harvesting was a job for two people. One person stood and poled the canoe. The other person sat and used sticks to knock the grains of rice into the canoe.

Peter always looked forward to the rice harvest. It was a time to play with his cousins. They also came to the lake with their parents.

On the third morning of harvesting, Peter awoke before anyone else. He dressed quickly. Outside, the sky was beginning to glow with the rising sun. Peter could see his breath in the chilly air. This was the morning he had been waiting for. Today, he would take a turn as Grandfather's ricing partner.

Peter and his grandfather slipped the canoe into the water. Peter stood with the tall pole. Grandfather sat in front of him.

"We'll start out slowly," said Grandfather. "Just push against the bottom."

Peter stuck the pole into the mud and pushed off. The canoe moved forward. It also tipped to one side. Peter steadied himself. Standing in a moving canoe was not easy.

"You've got the hang of it now," Grandfather told Peter after a while. The sun felt hot. Poling was hard work. But Peter felt good about the steady way he was moving the canoe.

While Peter steered, Grandfather used the sticks called *knockers*. He held a knocker in each hand. First he wrapped an arm and a stick around a bunch of stalks. Then he bent the stalks over the side of the canoe. Using the stick in his other hand, he knocked the tops of the stalks. The grains flew off. Most of them landed in the canoe bottom. Some landed in the water. Those would have a chance to make new plants for the next season.

Quickly, Grandfather used his other arm to grab another bunch. Again and again, Grandfather knocked with one stick, then the other. Peter listened to the *swish, rap, swish, rap.* It was like a song without words. The pile of rice grew larger.

When Grandfather suggested a break, Peter agreed right away. He was tired!

They rested and talked with friends. Then Peter and his grandfather switched places.

Peter tried using the knockers. At first, he couldn't get at the right part of the stalks. Then he knocked the grains everywhere but into the canoe. When they hit his face, they itched terribly. He kept trying, and slowly he improved.

It was nearly noon when Peter and his grandfather landed with a full canoe. They poured their rice into bags and headed home. It was time to "finish" the rice. There were still many steps to take.

First the rice was spread on plastic sheets.
The sun began to dry it out.

After that, the rice was stirred in a big metal
pot over a low fire. The rice dried more.

Then Grandfather "danced" on the rice.
Grind, grind, grind — slowly, the rice husks broke
away from the grains.

Next, the grains were tossed gently until the husk pieces blew away in the wind.

At last, the rice was ready to be cooked. Cooking was the easiest and fastest step of all.

The Ojibwe have many stories about the great hero Manabozho. Long, long ago, Manabozho's people used to go hungry during the cold winters. Manabozho prayed and fasted, but no dream came to show him how to help his people. Then, by a lake, Manabozho did have an important dream. He saw dancers swaying gracefully. He danced with them. When he awoke, he saw that the dancers were wild grasses. Birds came to eat the grains that fell from the grasses. Manabozho brought the good news to his people. Food was all around them, waiting to be harvested.

Now, there it was on Peter's family's table — the delicious wild rice called *manoomin*.

Responding

Think About the Selection

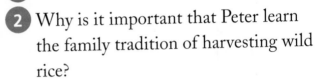

1. What do the Ojibwe call wild rice?

2. Why is it important that Peter learn the family tradition of harvesting wild rice?

3. What are the steps for harvesting wild rice?

Following Directions

Copy this chart on a piece of paper. Write directions that tell how to "finish" wild rice.

Directions for "finishing" wild rice

1. First the wild rice is spread on plastic sheets. The sun dries it.
2. ?
3. ?
4. ?
5. ?

21

Landslides

by Linda Hartley

What happens when tons of rocks and dirt slide down a mountain? **Monitor** your reading as you go. Reread to **clarify** parts that you don't understand.

A rock climber moves up the side of Washington Column.

It was a warm July evening in Yosemite National Park. A rock climber slowly made his way up Washington Column. Suddenly he heard a CRACK! "That sounds like thunder," he thought. But when he turned his head, there was no storm. The noise had come from the side of a nearby mountain.

CRACK! BOOM! Giant boulders bounced down the side of Glacier Point. "I just stood there with my mouth open," the rock climber said afterward.

Later he learned that 162,000 tons of rock had rushed down the mountain. They had traveled at about 160 miles an hour. Fourteen people were hurt. One person died. The rock climber had seen a huge landslide.

Inset: A landslide roars down a slope.

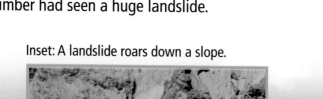

A landslide happens when large amounts of rocks and soil move from a high place to a lower place. Visitors to Yosemite don't often see landslides. A long time may pass between landslides. But the work of landslides can be seen all over Yosemite — and all over the world. For millions of years, landslides have changed the surface of the earth.

The view from Glacier Point
of Half Dome in Yosemite

Many landslides are caused by natural erosion. Wind and water wear away rocks and soil over time. Heavy rains and melting snow cause rocks and soil to loosen. If the land is steep, a landslide may happen. The landslide at Glacier Point was probably caused by natural erosion.

The two diagrams show what happens during a landslide.

Before

After

Geologists are people who study the earth. They know that landslides happen more often in some places than in others. Geologists look at rocks and soil and underground water. They measure slopes. They can often tell *where* a landslide is likely to happen. But geologists can't always tell *when* it will happen.

Most landslides are too fast, powerful, and dangerous to study in action. But there is one landslide of special interest. It moves very slowly, all the time. It is called the Slumgullion landslide. Its name means "watery meat stew."

Three scientists look down a landslide in the state of Washington.

The Slumgullion landslide in the 1800s

The Slumgullion landslide today

The huge Slumgullion landslide is in Colorado. Geologists can study how this landslide flows because it moves so slowly. Parts of the Slumgullion have been moving downward for 300 years. Like the fast landslide at Yosemite, this slow landslide is also caused by natural erosion.

Geologists use maps and photos to study landslides like the Slumgullion. Maps are made with the help of satellites circling the earth. Photos are taken from airplanes. Today's photos and maps are compared with old photos and maps. Geologists can see how the land has been changed.

Some landslides are caused by volcanoes. When a volcano erupts, tons of rocks and dirt can go flying down its sides. The volcano's power can create huge, deadly landslides.

In 1980 the Mount Saint Helens volcano in Washington erupted. A side of the mountain broke away in a great explosion. Lava and hot gases poured out. Ash, rocks, and soil formed a mighty landslide. It tore down millions of trees. Everything in the landslide's path was destroyed.

The Mount Saint Helens
volcano erupting in 1980

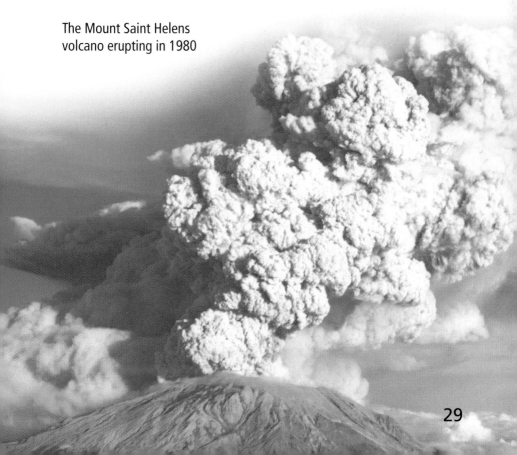

The Mount Saint Helens landslide seemed huge when it happened. But a landslide more than six times as large has been found underwater in the Atlantic Ocean. It happened many thousands of years ago. Its cause was an underwater volcano.

Underwater volcanoes have caused the largest landslides ever found. In the Pacific Ocean near Hawaii, scientists have found huge rock slides. Some of the rocks have moved over 100 miles from the volcanic mountain where they first fell. How did a landslide travel so far underwater? Scientists are still trying to find out.

Earthquakes are another force that can set off landslides. When large parts of the earth suddenly move, everything on the surface moves too. That is what happens in an earthquake. Rocks and soil are pushed loose from cliffs, roadsides, and slopes. All this stuff goes falling down as landslides.

The landslides caused by earthquakes are very powerful. In Montana in 1959, an earthquake caused an entire mountainside to slide into the Madison River.

By looking closely at areas where earthquakes often happen, geologists try to make predictions about landslides. They usually can tell where landslides are likely to happen in earthquake zones.

This gigantic crack in the earth was caused by an earthquake. The same power can cause large landslides.

Large fences are used to keep landslides from falling onto roads.

Natural erosion, volcanoes, and earthquakes all cause landslides. Some landslides, however, have a different cause — people. When people change the surface of the earth, landslides are often the result.

Landslides are possible on the sides of many roads because of the way the roads were built. Workers blast away hills to build roads. The blasting leaves steep slopes. The steeper the slopes, the greater the chance that rocks and soil will fall in a landslide. Road signs that say "Watch Out for Falling Rock" warn of the chance of a landslide.

Nowadays, road builders can do several things to prevent landslides. Sometimes they fix rocks in place with large bolts. Sometimes they use wire fences to keep falling rocks from landing on the road below. The important thing is to stop the rocks before they fall.

Clear-cutting can leave huge areas without trees.

Another way people cause landslides is by clear-cutting. Clear-cutting is the chopping down of all the trees in one area. This gets rid of the tree roots that once held rocks and soil in place. Without the roots, rain can then wash rocks and soil down slopes in a landslide. In Oregon, many people believe that landslides are getting worse because there is too much clear-cutting.

Landslides can be a big danger to houses built near hills. Many people enjoy living with beautiful views. So they live in houses on top of hills. But if a landslide happens, the ground can come out from under these homes. They can go sliding downhill. Or a landslide can send tons of rocks crashing down on houses at the bottom of hills.

Builders are finding new, safer ways to build near hills. They cut back into hillsides. Then they remove the loose rocks and soil that could slide into houses.

The houses on the side of this hill in Hollywood, California, could come crashing down if a landslide were to happen.

35

When engineers and builders make plans, they study the land. They get helpful information from geologists about where landslides might happen. They can then decide where to build — or not to build — roads, hospitals, homes, and schools.

As builders clear land for houses, the safest sites get used first. Before long, houses are built on areas that aren't safe. But geologists warn that some places are just too dangerous for building. Landslides can bury a house in moments. Even a beautiful view isn't worth being buried in a landslide.

The giant mudslide in the photo on the right ripped apart homes on this hill in California.

Geologists are always looking for new ways to study landslides. They get better at predicting where and when landslides might happen. By keeping track of landslides, geologists can protect people from these dangerous natural events.

A giant landslide at Red Mountain in the San Juan Mountains of Colorado

Some landslides are caused by changes people make to the earth's surface. Most are caused by erosion, volcanoes, and earthquakes. Either way, landslides are both terrible disasters and thrilling events that shape our ever-changing world.

Responding

Think About the Selection

1. What happens in a landslide?

2. What are two causes of landslides?

3. Give some supporting details that show how earthquakes make landslides happen.

Main Idea/Supporting Details

Copy this chart on a piece of paper. Write two supporting details for the second main idea.

Main Idea	Supporting Details
Many landslides are caused by natural erosion.	1. Wind and water wear away rocks and soil. 2. Rain and melting snow cause rocks and soil to loosen.
Geologists use maps and photos to study landslides.	1. ? 2. ?

WHITEOUT

by Kay Livorse
illustrated by Dave Kramer

Strategy Focus

Will a big blizzard bring big trouble for Mary Alice's family? As you read, try to **predict** what will happen next.

When Mary Alice woke up, she was startled by . . . silence. She heard no dogs barking, no traffic on the street. Where was the train whistle that usually woke her? Everything seemed so calm and quiet.

Mary Alice jumped up and looked out the window. Snow! Everywhere she looked. The whole world outside was white as . . . well, snow!

She ran into the next room to tell her brother Charlie the good news. She jumped on his bed to wake him up.

Mary Alice and Charlie raced downstairs. Mom and Robert were already making breakfast. Charlie headed for the door to the yard.

"Whoa!" said Robert. "Breakfast before play, Sport."

Robert was their stepfather. Their real father had died when Charlie was five. Mom had married Robert last year. Mary Alice had warmed to Robert right away. Charlie was still getting used to having someone in his dad's place.

"Great," said Charlie with a frown. "Look who made it home last night."

"Did you have trouble on the roads, Robert?" Mary Alice asked.

Robert had been a player for the Cleveland Browns football team. Now he was a police officer. He often worked late into the night.

"Got a ride just in time!" said Robert. "With all this snow, the roads will be closed for days. Plows can barely keep up."

44

Mom held up her hand. "Listen! They're talking about the storm on the radio," she said.

"Six hours into the blizzard and no end in sight. Folks, we've got a whiteout here. A record snowfall for eastern Ohio! People are warned to stay — " The radio went dead. The lights went out too.

"Yippee! Power's out!" said Charlie. "Who needs lights in the day, anyway?"

"Got plenty of coal in the cellar, though," Robert added. "At least the house'll keep warm."

But right now Mary Alice and Charlie didn't really care about a warm house. They had snowmen on their minds. They gobbled up their eggs and ran to the door.

"Mom, can we go out and play now?" Charlie asked.

"Sure," said Mom, "but dress warmly. Hats *and* mittens."

Mary Alice and Charlie dashed out the back door into the white swirl of snow.

"Stay in the yard," called Robert.

"Yes, boss," Charlie replied. The door slammed behind him.

Mary Alice had never seen such deep snow. She and Charlie flopped around in the drifts. They tried to build a snowman. They laughed and threw snowballs. Then Charlie headed toward the toolshed. He started to climb up on one side.

"Hey!" shouted Mary Alice. "What are you doing up there?"

"Look at me! I'm Super — " yelled Charlie. Before he finished the word, he jumped. He held his arms out like a superhero. But instead of flying, he flopped. Right into a huge drift of snow.

"Owwww!!" Charlie screamed from under a white pile. Mary Alice couldn't see him.

"Charlie!" cried Mary Alice. She tried to run to him. But the deep snow made it hard.

"My leg!" moaned Charlie. Now Mary
Alice could see her brother under the pile of
snow. He was crying and holding his right leg.

Robert rushed out the back door. He'd
heard Charlie's scream. He plowed through the
snow towards Charlie's red snow hat.

"What's the deal there, Sport?" he called to
Charlie. Robert could barely get through the
snow too. But he made it to Charlie before Mary
Alice.

Charlie saw Robert coming. "I'll be all
right," he said. "I don't need any help." He
tried to stand. His leg hurt so much he almost
passed out. He fell back into the snow.

Robert picked Charlie up and carried him into the house without a word. Mary Alice followed. She saw that Charlie was in too much pain to talk. She knew he didn't want to, anyway.

Robert took off Charlie's boots and gently felt his lower leg. Mary Alice could see that the limb was swollen. Tears filled Charlie's eyes.

Robert frowned. "Looks kind of like a broken leg there, Sport," said Robert. "Some ice on it will keep it from swelling more."

"I'll get a pan and fill it with snow," said
Mary Alice.

"Great idea," said Robert. "Snow will work
fine."

Mom tried to call the doctor, but the phone
was dead too. "What'll we do now?" she asked.

50

"Keep Charlie on ice," said Robert. "I'll walk to the police station. There's a hospital on the same street. I'll bet that street has been plowed. I'll find a doctor or something . . ."

"But that's miles away!" said Mary Alice. "How can you walk that far in this deep snow?"

Robert grinned and reached into the coat closet.

For a moment, Charlie forgot about his pain. "What are those things?" he asked.

"Snowshoes!" said Robert. "They let you walk in deep snow. Growing up in Vermont, I used my snowshoes all winter long."

They all watched Robert bundle up and strap on the snowshoes. Mary Alice thought he looked like he had tennis rackets on his feet.

"Be back with help in a jiff, Sport," Robert said to Charlie. "Everything'll be okay." Then he disappeared into the blowing white storm.

Mary Alice kept getting more snow for Charlie's leg. Mom made peanut butter sandwiches for lunch. Charlie tried not to think about his leg.

"Do you think Robert can get someone to help?" Charlie asked.

"Yes," said Mary Alice. "I think Robert can do just about anything."

Mom smiled and started to read them a mystery story to pass the time.

Mom was getting to the good part. Then, all of a sudden, they heard a rumbling noise outside. It was a snowplow, followed by an ambulance! Out of the plow jumped Robert.

Robert walked into the house with the ambulance driver. Mary Alice saw Charlie crack a small smile.

They all rode in the ambulance with Charlie. Mary Alice could see Charlie staring at Robert.

"You're not so bad after all," Charlie finally spoke up. "For a guy from Vermont."

Robert grinned and said, "Well, Charlie, I guess once you get to know me, I'm not all bad."

And the whole family smiled as the ambulance cut through the white walls of snow.

Responding

Think About the Selection

1. Where did Robert grow up?

2. When Mary Alice wakes up, why is she startled by the silence?

3. How can you tell that Charlie's feelings about Robert are changing?

Making Inferences

Copy this chart on a piece of paper. Then use the clues to make inferences.

What the author tells us:	What you can infer:
a. Mary Alice and Charlie race downstairs.	**a.** The children want to play in the snow.
b. "Great," said Charlie with a frown. "Look who made it home last night."	**b.** ?
c. Charlie tells Robert he doesn't need any help.	**c.** ?